# *About Dartmoor*

## Jack Whitton and Roy Westlake

## Bossiney Books • Launceston

First published 1998 by Bossiney Books, Langore, Launceston, Cornwall PL15 8LD
This reprint 2007
© 1998 Bossiney Books
All photographs are by Roy Westlake except those on pages 5,7 and 21 which
are by Paul White. The cover photograph shows Bowerman's Nose.
ISBN 978 1899383 14 6
Printed in Great Britain by R Booth Ltd, Mabe, Penryn, Cornwall TR10 9HH

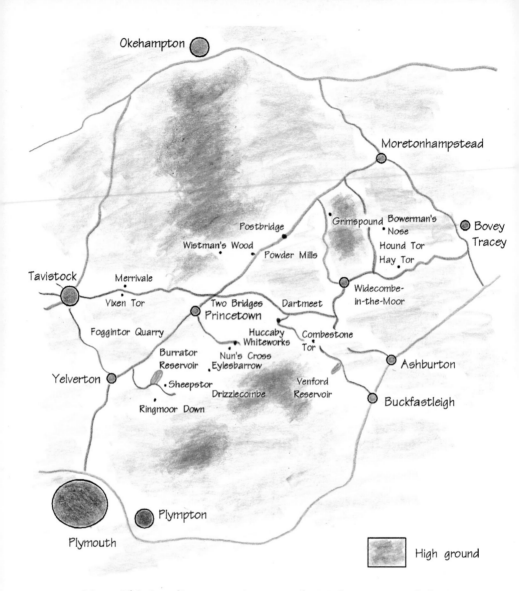

Okehampton

Moretonhampstead

Grimspound  Bowerman's
          • Nose                    ● Bovey
Postbridge        Hound Tor         Tracey
Wistman's Wood                      Hay Tor
           • Powder Mills

Tavistock      Merrivale
          Vixen Tor    Two Bridges   Dartmeet   Widecombe-
                       Princetown                in-the-Moor
     Foggintor Quarry      Huccaby   Combestone
                        Whiteworks   Tor
          Burrator     Nun's Cross                Ashburton
          Reservoir   Eylesbarrow
Yelverton       • Sheepstor           Venford
                Drizzlecombe         Reservoir   Buckfastleigh
          Ringmoor Down

                                              ███ High ground

Plympton

Plymouth

**Maps:** This is a diagrammatic map only. We have assumed that you have either the OS 1:25 000 Outdoor Leisure map 'Dartmoor', or the relevant 1:50 000 sheets, to find our recommended locations. It would be unwise to venture far from the road without such a map, and preferably a compass also. All map references are to the SX square.
**Warning:** Large areas north of the Tavistock-Moretonhampstead road are used by the Army for live firing. Our suggested walks avoid them.

*A frozen waterfall near Burrator. It can get very cold on Dartmoor! Even in summer the wind can make it colder than you expect – so go well prepared*

## Introduction

Dartmoor has some superb guidebooks, but they are mostly very detailed. This book will help you understand quickly and easily what there is to see, and give you carefully selected samples of each kind of feature.

The area covered is the higher and largely unenclosed part of the Moor, and we do not take you more than about 2km (1¼ miles) from the road. Some features can be seen without walking at all, and these are marked 🚗.

The features are grouped into four areas: Burrator (pages 4-10), Princetown (11-19), Dartmeet (20-24) and Widecombe (25-31). Each group might make a day out.

We suggest you need stout shoes and appropriate clothes. Be aware of possible weather changes, including low cloud, rain, and the chilling effect of wind on exposed hilltops. Don't walk on any bright green bogs and you'll be safe!

## Burrator Reservoir 🚗

This was created in 1898 to improve the supply of water to Plymouth. Until that time, an ancient leat built by Sir Francis Drake had supplied Plymouth from the River Meavy at this point. As was often the case with Drake, he rather confused his personal interest with that of the public, and diverted the original planned route in order to supply corn mills of his own.

Although little remains of Drake's Plymouth leat, the late eighteenth-century Devonport leat still flows, winding along the contours from near Princetown. By taking the narrow lane from the Reservoir up to Crossgate (562695) you can see beside the road the Devonport Leat, a medieval cross and, only 200m along the track, a well-marked cairn and cist – a Bronze age burial in a stone cist or chest, which was then covered with a cairn of stones. There is a pleasant and very easy round stroll from Crossgate to Leather Tor bridge (569699 – a clapper bridge of advanced design) and Norsworthy Bridge.

### Eylesbarrow mine

To the experienced eye, the remains of the tinners' activities, medieval streamworks, opencast works and spoil heaps are visible in many parts of the moor. The casual visitor will be more impressed by the remains of a later mine (which had underground workings) that are clearly visible at Eylesbarrow.

From the parking place at 577674, take the track which is a continuation of the road, past the left side of a conifer wood and steadily uphill. About 1100m from the wood, at 592676, the wall of the old smelting house still stands. This is thought to be the last place on Dartmoor where tin was smelted, until about 1831. Stamping houses (where ore was pulverised) and a wheel-pit can be seen, as well as dried up leats and spoil heaps.

Leats, many of which survive as drainage channels, were essential to the miners. Water was needed in the process of separating the ore from the spoil, and also to power the waterwheels which ran the stamping machines and drainage pumps. The reason why ruined engine houses are so rare on Dartmoor, compared with Cornwall, is that water was plentiful here and coal so difficult to transport to the mines that steam engines were uneconomic. Wheelpits are common, though because they are sunken features they are easy to miss.

Please take care if you explore the old mines anywhere. They are potentially dangerous. These hidden pits in the bracken and shafts capped two hundred years ago with timber now rotten are just two of the hazards.

A little further up from the smelting house wall, to the left of the track (at 597682), a series of paired stones run up the hill. These supported a horizontal flat-rod system which conveyed power from a water-wheel below to a pump 200m higher up the hill.

The more substantial buildings marked on the OS map include those of a farmhouse built about 1830: its 'newtake' walls can be found just south of the track. A newtake was a field enclosure reclaimed from the moor.

### Drizzlecombe stone rows and menhirs (593670)

As you return from Eylesbarrow, take the track down Drizzle Combe, then strike out across the river to explore the settlement, burial cairns, stone rows and menhirs (standing stones). This is one of the most remarkable ancient ceremonial complexes on Dartmoor, but it remains unclear in what order it was built. Probably the stone rows are Neolithic (c2000 BC) and older than the Bronze Age settlement (c1500 BC). The Neolithic people probably had wooden huts. The cairns and menhirs may have been a Bronze Age response to an earlier ancestral site.

It used to be thought that the developments of agriculture, metal-working and other technologies which divide the so-called Mesolithic, Neolithic, Bronze Age and Iron Age were each the result of invasions by a new people, bringing novel ideas from the Mediterranean and Near East. Archaeologists are now sceptical about this: new ideas may have been copied from neighbouring peoples, brought by travelling metal-workers, or even simultaneously invented in several places. Steam engines and computers both spread around the world without massive population movements, and international trade was much greater in prehistoric times than most people realise.

The Bronze Age people may have believed that the stone rows had been built by their own ancestors – and they in turn were probably among the ancestors of today's Devonians, not some alien people later eliminated by technological superiors.

Whilst future archaeological digs may yet throw some light on the order in which the elements of the site at Drizzlecombe were built, we shall never know what religious meaning the place had for the ancient farmers here – though this has never stopped people guessing, or even inventing 'ancient' fertility rituals. The largest Drizzlecombe menhir (opposite) was measured before being re-erected in 1893 as 17ft 10in (6.5m).

Incidentally, most of these ancient stones were re-erected in Victorian times, not necessarily in their original position, which makes the search for astronomical alignments a fruitless task – but the human mind always seeks patterns and, with a little ingenuity, generally finds them.

### Sheepstor village (560676) 🚗

Just south of Burrator reservoir, this picturesque village nestles below the tor after which it is named.

The church has several interesting features. There is an old cross outside the gate, and St Leonard's Well is beside the road east of the churchyard. (Go through the churchyard, through the kissing gate and another gate, turn right down the lane and it's 20m on the right.)

Looking out from the porch, some 20m away, beside a private gated stile, is another stumpy cross, and also an 'inch-hole'. This stone was once set in the side of a leat, and allowed a limited amount of water to be drawn off by the neighbouring

farmer. Enlarging the hole was strictly forbidden.

Within the church you will find interesting old memorials, including one to Sir Francis Drake's sister-in-law and her husband, and the extraordinary story of Rajah Brooke, the white rajah of Sarawak, who is buried in the churchyard with other members of his family.

A very fine view of the village and the reservoir can be had, without even leaving your car, from Ringmoor Down (559669) or rather more energetically by climbing Sheeps Tor. You may even find the Pixies' cave.

**Merrivale stone rows (555748)**

This ritual complex is much nearer the road than Drizzlecombe. One of the nicest approaches is from the Four Winds car park (561749) where there was once a school. Go through the back of the car park and turn right along the leat behind it. This leads to the stone rows, which date from perhaps 2000 BC.

Associated with the two double rows are cairns, which may be the same age or possibly later, a cist without any cairn, and to the south a stone circle and another line of cairns. Between the upper end of the rows and the road are numerous hut circles, presumed to be Bronze Age (perhaps 1500 BC) and an object identified by a Victorian antiquarian as a 'cromlech' or chambered tomb. To his embarassment it was subsequently identifed as a crushing stone for cider apples, which due to some defect was never collected from where it had been made.

### The Princetown Railway

First opened in 1823 as a mineral line called the Plymouth and Dartmoor Railway, it was only later extended to Princetown, where the station was at 418 m (1373 ft). The Yelverton to Princetown section, looping crazily around the hillsides to minimise the gradients, was one of the most scenic railway journeys in England, and most of it can still be walked. (The gravelly track might be possible for some wheelchairs.) There are branches into each of the quarries on the route.

It brought late Victorian tourists (including Sir Arthur Conan Doyle) to Princetown, 'the capital of the Moor', but was a casualty of the motor age and closed in 1956.

## Foggintor Quarry (567736)

This can be reached either by way of the Princetown Railway track from Princetown, or from the car park at 568749. (Access on foot past Yellowmeade Farm is permitted, cars are not.)

The quarry worked, under the name Royal Oak, from about 1820 to about 1900, although the nearby Swell Tor quarry was worked later than this, and the Merrivale quarry (opened in 1875) worked until very recently, producing a particularly high quality granite.

As well as the workings themselves, you will find the remains of numerous buildings at Foggintor, and you may well find climbers (often from the Army) scaling its rock faces.

### Vixen Tor (542743)

Visible from the road near Merrivale, this was the legendary home of a witch named Vixana. Before the road was made, in the 1770s, a track led across the moor from Tavistock to Ashburton. Vixen Tor was a landmark on it. Just west of Vixen Tor the path twisted through a bog, and Vixana lurked there waiting for travellers. By her spells she created mists, which swirled around her victims until they were disorientated, lost the path and were sucked down into the bog.

She was finally defeated by a traveller with a magic ring. (Perhaps he was also carrying a copy of *The Hobbit*.) If you choose to walk to the tor, don't say you weren't warned...

## Dartmoor Prison 🚗

The chilling presence of the prison is very much a feature of the Moor and perhaps for some tourists a macabre attraction. It was built to house prisoners of the wars with Napoleon, and it held no fewer than 7000 prisoners and 500 soldiers to guard them. There was no heating, and water ran down the inside of the walls, but conditions were better than on the prison hulks previously used. Americans as well as French were imprisoned here, because Britain went to war with the USA in 1812, and there were also many British sailors who on principle refused to fight the Americans. One in ten died in custody.

After the war the prison was deserted for thirty years, till the Australians refused to accept any more convicts and in 1850 the prison was reopened for civilian prisoners. During the First World War most of the prisoners were volunteered into the armed forces and a new generation of 'conchies' arrived.

Nowadays the prison facilities are greatly improved, and with today's gaol population crisis there is no prospect of closure.

## Wistman's Wood

This is one of the most extraordinary features on the Moor, and it is an easy walk of about 2 km (1¹/₄ miles) each way. At Two Bridges there is public parking space for about 20 cars opposite the Hotel (609750). Follow the signposted track north to Crockern farmhouse, round it to the right, and then follow the signposts till you leave the enclosed farmland. From this point you can see the wood ahead of you.

It is a long thin wood of oaks, all growing from a 'clitter' or jumble of stones, and consequently gnarled and stunted, though they are now much taller than at any time in the last four centuries. Trees and boulders are covered with mosses and lichen, including the distinctive *Bryoria smithii*; it grows in only one other site in Britain, being extremely sensitive to pollution.

The name Wistman's Wood has provoked much speculation. William Crossing (1847-1928), who devoted his life to Dartmoor studies, had heard the old men of the moor refer to it as Welshman's wood. The Saxons referred to all the old Celtic speakers as *wealas*, and this may be the origin. Perhaps the most likely is the dialect word 'wisht', which means weird, affected by magic, perhaps haunted.

Certainly the wood is weird enough, especially at twilight, when legend says that the Devil hunted the moor with his pack of wisht hounds, looking for sinners. The hounds were particularly fond of Wistman's Wood, where they drove their prey to take cover, but where the poor hunted human would break his legs scurrying through the boulders, and die of terror, before being carried off to the infernal domaine... Could the 'wisht man' be a euphemism for the Devil himself?

Antiquarians of the eighteenth century, that so-called Age of Reason, were convinced that the Druids had a hand in everything, and for them Wistman's Wood was an oak grove in which white-robed priests severed the golden bough with flint knives.

Modern archaeologists, more interested in pollen deposits than in mistletoe, tell us that Dartmoor was generally wooded until perhaps 5000 BC, when the earliest farmers began to use slash-and-burn techniques to make clearings in the forest, so starting a lengthy process from which the present peat bogs and treeless landscape evolved. The wood is one small remnant of the ancient forest, accidentally preserved because the clitter in which it grows makes it worthless for agriculture.

And yet... The wood lies just downhill from numerous ancient hut-circles. Perhaps it was indeed spared as a magic grove, tended by a colony of priests?

Druid fantasy or scientific scepticism, you can take your pick, but either way it makes a delightful short walk.

*Below: Nun's Cross and the deserted Nun's Cross Farm*

## Whiteworks (612710) 🚗 and Nun's Cross (605699)

A lane out of Princetown leads to this group of cottages and the extensive remains of the abandoned Whiteworks tin mine. Two other features are immediately noticeable. The Devonport leat (see page 5) winds its way across this desolate landscape before disappearing into a 592 m (648 yd) tunnel. Directly in front of the cottages lies the Fox Tor Mire, immortalised in *The Hound of the Baskervilles* as the Great Grimpen Mire. The OS map shows a theoretical path across it, but it is not recommended.

A short walk from Whiteworks brings you to Nun's Cross, also known as Siward's Cross. This is at least 760 years old and probably more. It marks both a property boundary and also a cross-roads on the ancient system of tracks across the moor, including the Abbot's Way from Buckfast to Tavistock, with a branch to Buckland – or 'Bocland' as the stone has it.

*Of the many examples of clapper bridges on the Moor, this one on the old 'post road' at Postbridge is probably the finest, with its triple span and pointed cutwaters*

## Postbridge clapper bridge (648789) 🚗

The earliest way of crossing rivers was of course to ford them, and bridges are often on the site of earlier fords. Later came stepping stones, and a natural progression from stepping stones was to lay either timbers or stones between them. There is no way of telling how old the present structures are. Some may be medieval, but they have almost all had to be repaired within modern times following storm damage. A large tree carried down by storm water can easily knock off the horizontal stone.

This particular bridge suffered an indignity about 1825 when a young farmer deliberately pushed one of the centre stones off the piers on the upstream side, trying to make it fall vertically against the piers. His intention was to dam the river to create a duck-pond! Fortunately he was a bad engineer and the stone fell flat into the river rather than edgewise, which made him abandon the project. He lived long enough to see it replaced, in 1880, but apparently in the wrong position – 'upside down and inside out', as one old man expressed it.

## Powder Mills 🚗

Halfway between Postbridge and Two Bridges, the old powder mills lie just north of the B3212. There is a pottery at Powder Mills Farm which is in itself well worth visiting. The pots are very simple, often inspired by medieval shapes, and wood-fired using Japanese techniques.

The buildings here once housed workers at the mills, which flourished from 1844 to 1900, when dynamite rapidly ousted gunpowder from the quarries and mines. At their peak, these works employed a hundred men, and the hamlet included a chapel and a school.

The advantage of Dartmoor for this industry was that land was cheap, so the buildings housing the various processes could be widely scattered. Explosions were an ever present danger, and the walls were made extremely thick, with a very light roof, so that any blast went upwards taking the roof with it.

## Hexworthy, or Huccaby, Bridge 🚗

This is one of the most picturesque spots on the Moor, close to the 'Ancient Tenement' of Huccaby. The 'Ancient Tenements' were farms so old that they predated the creation of the 'Forest' of Dartmoor, probably in the time of William the Conqueror. They had certain rights not shared by later farms which were enclosed out of the Forest lands.

The word 'Forest' here has nothing to do with woodland. It was a legal term for hunting land owned by the king, in which special very harsh laws applied. Only certain parts of the Dartmoor area – mainly the central part – became a Forest, and all this Forest area was made a part of the parish of Lydford. Because only the sovereign can own a forest, when in 1206 Dartmoor Forest was granted by the king to his brother, it was technically deafforested and became a 'Chase'.

There is no need for abrupt change in such matters, so for the time being it continues to be known as 'the Forest'!

*Early morning near Dartmeet, close by Huccaby*

### The Forest Inn and Jolly Lane Cot 🚗

A few hundred metres south from the bridge is the ancient Forest Inn, but just before you reach it you pass Jolly Lane Cot which was built in a single day, in 1835. There was an ancient tradition that if a house could be built on common land in a single day, a plot enclosed and a fire lit in the hearth, the builder acquired a right to the land. This house was the last to be thrown together under those conditions.

It must have required great organisation, the help of many friends, and the brief absence of the local farmer, to achieve it. The builders started at one end, so that they were thatching one end of the roof before the other end wall was completed.

### Combestone Tor (670718) 🚗

This attractive tor stands right beside the road, and appeals to youngsters wanting to let off steam playing round the rocks. The views northwards are spectacular. Notice the stripes on the opposite hillside, Yartor. They are 'reaves', the remains of land boundaries dating back to about 1500 BC.

These huge field systems, involving reaves running in straight lines for many kilometres, sometimes making long parallel fields, divided the central common grazing land from the possessions of each Bronze Age 'parish', and then subdivided land within the parish. The reaves themselves were broad and low, probably only 40-50 cm, around 18 in, in height. Hedge plants would have been planted down the middle.

If you want to see one of them close up, turn your back on the tor, cross the road, and head due south: 500 m from the road you will cross the reave. (On your way you may notice hut circles and a cairn, also Bronze Age.) This reave is marked on the OS map as 'boundary work'. You may also want to look at Horn's Cross, and search for the stone rows: most of the stones are very low, so can be hidden under the bracken in summer.

## Grimspound (701809)

This site is one you absolutely must visit. There are something over 5000 hut circles on Dartmoor, most of them Bronze Age and many of them clustered in villages, but the Grimspound 'village' stands out because (as a result of some restoration a century ago) the walls stand higher. The climate was warmer in the Bronze Age than it is today, and the soil not yet exhausted. The people who lived here around 3300 years ago herded animals, grew crops (probably oats and beans) and perhaps 'streamed' for tin in the valley below. Some of the 'hut circles' were animal shelters rather than dwellings.

Bronze is an alloy of tin and copper, and the tin of Dartmoor was probably first worked at this time, in a method rather like panning for gold. This continued to be the favoured method until at least Tudor times. Look slightly to the right across the valley from Grimspound and you will see among the bracken 'openworks' or 'gerts' – long pits from which tin was dug in perhaps the 18th century. Now look slightly to the left, where there are grass fields. These once belonged to the medieval village of Challacombe, now shrunk to a few houses.

### Hound Tor and its medieval settlement (746788)

After the Bronze Age, there is little evidence of human habitation in the higher parts of the moor until late Saxon times. Presumably farming was easier in the lower lands, with better soils and a softer climate, so that the moor was only resettled when the pressures of a rising population made it necessary. Such pressures became acute about AD1200.

The site was deserted around 1350, partly because the weather was deteriorating from about 1300, but also because of the Black Death. Even if the inhabitants themselves survived, upland farmers could step into dead lowland shoes, and many hill farms were deserted at this time, never to be reoccupied. If you look around, you will see modern pasture fields not much lower than Hound Tor village, but no one tries to grow crops at 340m (1100ft).

From the middle of the main car park (739792) head for the tor. You don't need to climb it unless you want to: just keep slightly to the right of it, and once you are over the crest you will see Greator Rocks ahead of you. Head for the lower end of Greator and you should find the settlement. From Greator, you get a good view of the medieval field system, in which the characteristic ridge and furrow marks are visible.

Although there are a number of buildings, it is thought that there were only four houses, and later just three. The rest are outbuildings. The largest of them (nearest Greator) was the manor house. There is a cross-passage in the middle: the family lived in the 'hall' uphill from the passage, with a hearth, and the animals lived in the room below the passage, with a drain leading through the wall. Later an inner room was added to the hall. The squire and his family, not to mention his cows, must have been very snug in here, though their Bronze Age predecessors would have thought it very unhygienic!

It is not difficult to identify with these medieval people, despite their obvious poverty and squalor. For a dozen generations they fought a losing battle here to make a livelihood from the Moor.

### Haytor

Haytor is very popular because it is the most massive outcrop of granite on the moor, has stupendous views, and also has interesting industrial relics. The rocks themselves, and the car park, can become rather crowded in summer, but you can still avoid the crowds.

Park in the car park (758767). Head up to the right of the outcrop. At 759771 you will find a path leading down hill (north-east). Descend it until you come to another track crossing it. A left turn here takes you to a wooden gate in a wire fence. Inside this fence is Haytor quarry, surprisingly quiet and (if the wind is as biting as when I was last there one January) relatively warm and sheltered. From this quarry came stone for London Bridge and the British Museum library. It worked from 1819 to the 1860s, and was briefly revived on later occasions.

Dartmoor quarries all had problems getting the stone to their markets, and at Haytor the remarkable solution – obvious

in retrospect – was a tramway made from the granite itself, much of which is still visible today. Iron rails frequently broke in 1820, steel was not available, and granite was the best option as well as being on the spot.

Leave the quarry by the wooden gate, rejoin the path you were on, and in about 100m turn left along the track of the tramway. Its various branches are clearly marked on the maps, and you can explore as much of them as you have time for.

The wagons used on the tramway had four wheels, with no flanges (thus making it a 'tramway' rather than a 'railway'). Each carried around three tonnes. At one point (753777) loaded wagons were required to go uphill, and a team of 18 carthorses pulled the train over this stretch. After that it was downhill all the way – 390m (1300ft) in the 13.5km (8$^{1}/_{2}$ miles) to Teigngrace, where there was a canal.

It is possible to circle right round Haytor rocks, back to the car park.

**Bowerman's Nose (742804)** 🚗

This freak of nature stands some 12 m high. Legend has it that Bowerman lived about AD 1100. He mischievously disturbed a coven of witches, and was turned to stone in revenge.

## Widecombe

Widecombe is superbly situated, very beautiful, and very famous! It is appropriately known for the song 'Widecombe Fair', which celebrates Uncle Tom Cobley and rather too many other people trying to get onto one spot – in their case, the back of a horse. At the height of the season it gets extremely busy, so you'll enjoy this delightful place far more if you can visit it at some quieter time.

The church was famously struck by lightning during a service in 1638, when four people were killed and 62 injured. A contemporary account is preserved inside the tower. Folklore naturally attributes the blame to the devil, who was chasing one sinner in particular, but didn't mind laying into a few more while he was at it.

### The ponies 🚗

Wherever you go on the moor, you are likely to see ponies. They graze on the common land of Dartmoor along with sheep and cattle, and although they are wild, they are in fact the property of farmers. Under no circumstances should you feed them, as this encourages them near the roads where each year many are killed, especially at night.

Every autumn there is the annual 'drift' at which all the ponies are herded together and sorted out between their various owners. Some are sold at auction. Others are branded and returned to the Moor. Very few of them these days are purebred 'Dartmoor ponies'. The ancient pure breed is particularly hardy, and there are attempts to improve the present stock so that they do not suffer in severe winters.

The pony population is the subject of much debate in Devon, especially among the breeders, farmers and the RSPCA.